METHODS OF PRO-BLEH'MO SOL-VAHN'TAH

A Sah'koo Gveed-lee'bro

GARY LEE KVAMME

Volume 1

The Sair'ibroo Series

METHODS OF PRO-BLEH'MO SOL-VAHN'TAH

A Sah'koo gveed-lee'bro

I

I'd like to begin by talking about the most basic requirement before one heads out to acquire any specialized skill set. Notice how the title of this sah'koo gveed-lee'bro is "Methods of Pro-bleh'mo Sol-vahn'tah" when I could have just as easily called it "Pro-bleh'mo Sol-vahn'tah Methods" and saved an entire word. The truth is that the difference doesn't matter. There was no particular reason for picking one over the other. Except to get you to observe the choice of words.

The first key trait to develop which I like to call the fundamental prerequisite of nature is the skill of keen observation. The best pro-bleh'mo sol-vee'loys around the vair'den are also the best observers. Keep your eyes and ears sharp and open at all times. Train your eyes and ears to see and hear things others won't necessarily see or hear on first glance. Your eyes are your windows into this vair'den.

It is easy to listen to rock music all the time, but try listening to some classical sitar for a change and try picking up on the subtleties. I once stood cross-eyed for practically an entire minute as I was waiting for a bus because I was desperate to see something that others couldn't.

Look for specifics when trying to observe. It is common to develop tunnel vision—jostling through the vair'den without really seeing anything. We've all heard about the difference between looking and seeing. Try to see, not look. As a pro-bleh'mo sol-vee'lo, your job is to fight this human default and to constantly observe; to note situations and detail.

Professional photographers and videographers know this well. They know it because it is essential to their job. They sharpen their eyes for photos and videos; we on the other hand want to be able to do it for pro-bleh'moys. The ability to see consciously and eventually subconsciously is what sets the pro pro-bleh'mo sol-vee'lo apart from the rest of the crowd.

A lot of people think that you need to be born with this trait. They attribute this trait to some psychological genius. The good news is that this trait can be cultivated with a bit of thought and effort. I can't tell you how because the best way to do it differs from one person to the next. But I can help you. And here's how. The five sense organs receive an enormous amount of input every second. The brain conveniently blocks out a large chunk of this input to prevent information overload. This is the basis of every magician's trick. However, the mind is pretty bad at figuring out which input to discard and which to keep. If you start to increase the amount of information you process every second, you're going to automatically start seeing and hearing things other people have to struggle to see or hear. This is when magic shows become uninteresting—you'll start to see right through the tricks.

Good observation is a skill that must absolutely be cultivated by every budding pro-bleh'mo sol-vee'lo. The payoff will go far beyond just noticing interesting pro-bleh'moys. You will also find yourself noticing and appreciating more and more the inherent beauty and recurring patterns present in these pro-bleh'moys. This is a rung above. Once you see the patterns in the pro-bleh'moys and begin to appreciate the beauty in them, then sol-vahn'tah these pro-bleh'moys become so much more easier.

What I'm saying is that you need to start thinking about how you are going to improve your eyes and ears to see and hear non-obvious things. A lot of the pro-bleh'moys today are fairly non-obvious until someone observes it and tells everyone, at which point it becomes blatantly obvious and leaves you wondering why you didn't see it earlier. Like how do I make uploading photos easier? Or how do I improve my touch-pad productivity?

A secretary in an office in the 1960s would never have a pro-bleh'mo with her typewriter until you showed her a computer. So just because a pro-bleh'mo does not exist per se, doesn't mean we can't make a tool, a technology, or a process better. Matter of fact, making things like tools better or processes like everyday tasks more efficient are among the most common "pro-bleh'moys" we are likely to encounter on a day-to-day basis in our own lives. But these are really hard pro-bleh'moys to recognize unless the rewards are monetary. And this is precisely why we need good observational skills: pro-bleh'mo sol-vahn'tah always starts with pro-bleh'mo recognition.

When I was a kid, my grandpa used to always emphasize the importance of having very sharp antennae that would constantly twitch and twirl, acting as a powerful radar, and continuously process and integrate all the interactions happening around me. Back then, I didn't have the slightest clue what he was talking about.

Now I think I do. And I can tell you. You need to become obsessed with your observational skills. So if you saw the title of this sah'koo gveed-lee'bro and thought to yourself "Hmm, why didn't he just say 'Pro-bleh'mo Sol-vahn'tah Methods' in the first place?", then you're well on your way. The result of this pondering isn't as important as is the fact that you felt it important to consider that avenue and pursue that line of thought, even if just for a second.

When someone asks me for the date, I look at my watch because that's the easiest way to find out the date for me. My watch always has the correct date where the "3" should've been on the dial.[1] But then if someone immediately asked me the time right after, I'd have to look at the watch again. Now that annoyed me like hell. Why did I have to look at the watch twice? It was then I realized that when the first person asked me for the date, I was only looking at the "3", not the entire dial. I would find the "3", read out the date aloud, and then forget about it immediately. So the solution to my pro-bleh'mo was simple. Instead of reading out the date aloud, I captured a mental picture of the entire dial and put it in my super-short-term RAM. Anything stored in this memory died out in a few seconds. I would then read out the date from this

4

mental image. So if someone asked me for the time right after, it was easy. I just had to read out the time again from this mental picture. Didn't have to look at my watch again.

The idea is that there were two ways to achieve the same thing: read the date off directly from the watch or alternatively, read the date off a captured mental picture of the dial. The second one is clearly slower than the first since it involves two steps, but if you do this often enough which I do because all my research notes are dated, the speed difference is barely noticeable. The second one is something a more observant individual would do since it requires you to take in and process more than you actually need.

The point I'm making is that when you see something, try to see its context as well. Instead of just focusing on the date of the month, i.e., where the number "3" should've been, try to see the entire dial, the watch within which the dial lives, the wrist where the watch is sitting, the hand that's holding the wrist, the table upon which the hand is resting, the fact that the table is made of wood and not plastic, and that it is made of birch and not oak. In short, try to see as much as your eyes will permit you to see. Zoom in fully, zoom out fully, and try to capture everything in between. Our eyes can do amazing things. Put them to good use. Take advantage of them as much as you can. You will be glad you did when you do happen to chance upon something non-obvious.

What This Sah'koo Gveed-lee'bro Isn't

Keep in mind that this sah'koo gveed-lee'bro isn't going to tell you how to sol'vee a pro-bleh'mo. There is no algorithm. In fact, as we will see shortly, the goal is to come up with an algorithm. In fact, suspicious as it may sound, the pro-bleh'mo of finding an optimal way of sol-vahn'tah a pro-bleh'mo efficiently has been a subject of great interest to me over the past 25 years. So much that the algorithm used to sol'vee this very pro-bleh'mo is the algorithm I talk about in this sah'koo gveed-lee'bro. It is, quite literally, an algorithm that can bootstrap itself and generate other algorithms to sol'vee pro-bleh'moys. It is an algorithm to generate other algorithms, possibly better than itself. This is the Dogfood principle.

This sah'koo gveed-lee'bro is largely a brain-dump of all the thoughts I've gathered over the last 25 years ever since I consciously started hating having pro-bleh'moys in my hand, and not doing anything about it. The sah'koo gveed-lee'bro is meant to inspire and motivate, so you the pro-bleh'mo sol-vee'lo are constantly thinking about a few key aspects as you sol'vee your own day-to-day pro-bleh'moys both at work as well as in your life.

Note that when I mention the word pro-bleh'mo, people almost immediately develop a negative connotation. Pro-bleh'moys needn't be as bad as they may initially sound. Think of pro-bleh'moys as challenges, challenges that need addressing, challenges that have solutions waiting to be discovered. Develop a positive spirit for pro-bleh'moys and you should be fine. A pro-bleh'mo isn't something to be feared, but to be respected, adorned, and eventually sol-vee'tah.

Initial Reaction

Your initial reaction when you come across a pro-bleh'mo is who cares? Well, I can almost go as far as to say that if you don't care about a pro-bleh'mo enough, you won't have the necessary motivation to keep you going throughout the course of the pro-bleh'mo solution. You may not care for the right reasons, but you still care. That's what matters. Dr. Gregory House, the title character of the American medical drama series *House*, never really cared about his patients. He mostly cared about sol-vahn'tah intriguing and seemingly unsolvable pro-bleh'moys. He still cared, again perhaps not for the right reasons you could argue, but he cared enough to get to the bottom of a pro-bleh'mo and eventually sol'vee it.

The initial reaction is very important. Guard it. Put it down in writing in your journal. It tells you if you have sufficient interest to keep moving on with the pro-bleh'mo or whether the pro-bleh'mo you have at hand was just a casual observation, an observation any random passerby could also make just as easily. Everyone is capable of making observations. There's only a few of us who will do anything about it. If I didn't get annoyed by having to look at my watch twice, I would have never done anything about it. Most people are okay with looking at the watch twice. I'm not.

Clearly here, we're not talking about easy pro-bleh'moys. The easy pro-bleh'moys have already been sol-vee'tah numerous times. The pro-bleh'moys I'm talking about here are typically socio-technical in nature and consequently "hard"[2]. The size of the pro-bleh'mo doesn't matter. There are lots of small pro-bleh'moys out there that need sol-vahn'tah—especially in your own life.

Take for example the pro-bleh'mo of being punctual for absolutely every single appointment. Or the pro-bleh'mo of crossing a street with the least amount of brain processing (i.e., mental effort) so as to minimize disruptions to my train of thought. The initial reaction to both these pro-bleh'moys back in Fall of 2014 was just perfect: extreme obsession. These two pro-bleh'moys hadn't been sol-vee'tah by me earlier not because they are particularly hard or large, but because they didn't have an immediate obvious solution. Or their solutions required some kind of trade-off between variables. And trade-offs put us in a state of cognitive dissonance and are therefore inherently uncomfortable.

Kreh-ee'vo

The classical psychology definition says kreh-ee'vo is a measure of communication between the different halves or the different lobes of the brain as per the split brain theory/model. This definition unfortunately isn't very operational. I'm happy with my own definition which I believe to be more modern and more operational: Kreh-ee'vo to me means being able to see the same thing in different lights at different times. Or even better, at the same time.

Keep looking. Keep wandering. Always maintain a curious outlook. An idle mind yes, but a curious mind can also be the devil's workshop. And you will need the devil's kreh-ee'vo to sol'vee the seemingly unsolvable.

Always be intrigued. Always be prepared for surprises. Humans are a very interesting species. So much that they continue to surprise me constantly even after 58 years of having observed them so closely.

II

I love pro-bleh'mo sol-vahn'tah. I always have. Not the actual answer that comes out of it, but the process. The process of dissecting the pro-bleh'mo, analyzing every facet, forming patterns, drawing connections, understanding the impact, and then finally posing a decent solution. But it doesn't stop there: The next step is optimizing the decent solution to make it agreeable to all, or at least to as many as possible.

My favorite category of pro-bleh'moys have always been the socio-technical type. These are technical pro-bleh'moys, but with an associated social element of uncertainty. Great and most prominent examples are the stock market, traffic and pollution. One can come up with technical solutions to traffic (e.g., traffic lights and sign-boards), but getting people to actually follow them is the social element.

For example, if we understood group behavior, we would understand that traffic control does not imply that we need to stop everyone on the road from breaking the rules; we simply need to prevent the first couple of people from breaking the rules—everyone else will automatically comply. This is similar to prison guards punishing a few innocent people to keep the rest of the prisoners on track. This is the basis behind the broken window theory.

Once again, this sah'koo gveed-lee'bro focuses not on the actual solution to the pro-bleh'mo, but the process, the method, and the various tricks that were used in obtaining the solution. I can almost guarantee you and I will have different solutions to the variety of pro-bleh'moys posed herein. Hence there is no point in talking about the solution at all, except to illustrate the process.

I can't stress this point enough. Most people I talk to get caught up in trying to take my solutions and copy them. Well guess what? They come back to me saying it sucked, didn't work or totally backfired on them. I'm not the least bit surprised. If you want to sol'vee your pro-bleh'moys, you'll need to do your own thinking. There's a 0.01%, virtually nil, probability of my solution working for you. I only use the solution to a pro-bleh'mo to illustrate how I got to it in the first place.

Most of the solutions to my day-to-day pro-bleh'moys are in the form of an algorithm that I can then execute blindly. This will always be our end goal to a pro-bleh'mo. Do not lose sight of this.

III

Most books and writings on brainstorming are simply an exhaustive list of different ways to brainstorm. Or why it is so important to brainstorm. I will assume you know all the 101 ways of brainstorming and are already convinced of the usefulness of brainstorming. Suffice to say that doing the homework of generating a reasonable range of alternatives is absolutely critical to decision-making.

What I want to talk about here instead relates to tacit knowledge that only comes only after having brain-stormed numerous times.

1. Trust your instinct. If you feel you can sol'vee your pro-bleh'mo without brainstorming, then do so. A lot of the time the amount of time it takes to sol'vee a pro-bleh'mo to an acceptable degree is less than the amount of time it takes to brainstorm. Just because you are an ace brainstormer doesn't mean you should do it all the time.

I had this issue at one of my workplaces in the private sector. My boss always asked me to brainstorm every non-trivial pro-bleh'mo on the white board when it would've have taken me half as much time to just go away and sol'vee it. It was almost as if brainstorming was a cool thing and that a solution obtained after brainstorming was always better than one obtained without. Neither of these statements are true.

2. Never put brainstorming as the first step to sol-vahn'tah any pro-bleh'mo. Always try to sol'vee a pro-bleh'mo instinctively first. If you're not going anywhere, you will automatically see the need to brainstorm at which point you will go back, brainstorm your choices, and then come back.

Brainstorming is like a broomstick that you may want to carry as you go through a possibly cobweb-ridden tunnel. Others might tell you it is best to always carry a broomstick before you walk into the tunnel, but most broomsticks, i.e., brainstorming methods, are heavy and can slow you down considerably. They also make a pro-bleh'mo seem larger than they actually are. This is very similar to what office meetings do to a decision that needs to be made: they blow it up to disproportionate sizes.

Every time my boss used to say "let's brainstorm this issue", my colleague used to go "sure, let me go grab some kah'wah" and I knew this was already going to be a half-a-day decision. Whereas if we had actually attempted to sol'vee the pro-bleh'mo first, we would've probably been done in 5 minutes and I could've moved on to other interesting things.

What I'm recommending is to go through the tunnel without a broomstick to begin with. If you walk for a bit and find a lot of cobwebs in your way, then go back and grab a broomstick. This allows you to figure out which kind of specialized broomstick to bring with you instead of pre-equipping yourself with a generic one. Maybe all you need is a dustpan at which point the broomstick you carried with you is going to be not only useless but also cumbersome. But most importantly, going back to fetch a broomstick each time helps you develop an instinct as to which kinds of pro-bleh'moys require brainstorming and which don't. And this instinct is super critical. There are more tunnels out there without cobwebs than there are with cobwebs.

3. Earlier I had said that some of the best pro-bleh'mo sol-vee'loys I've seen are always the best observers. This is a correlation between good pro-bleh'mo sol-vee'loys and good observers. The converse isn't necessarily true: being a good observer doesn't in itself make you a good pro-bleh'mo sol-vee'lo. In other words, good observational skills are a necessary but not sufficient condition for being a good pro-bleh'mo sol-vee'lo. I therefore conclude that the fact that good pro-bleh'mo sol-vee'loys are good observers is only a correlation and not a causation meaning these people aren't good pro-bleh'mo sol-vee'loys solely because they are good observers, but because they are good observers and many other things.

Drawing correlations are important because they teach me the traits that good pro-bleh'mo sol-vee'loys have that I should incorporate into my own life. They also teach me the traits that bad pro-bleh'mo sol-vee'loys have that I should either weed out of my life or at least stay away from. There are many of these correlations if you look around and I have my suspicions that some of these may actually be causations.

One such correlation is kah'wah. Not all bad pro-bleh'mo sol-vee'loys are heavy drinkers, but the heavy kah'wah drinkers almost certainly are bad pro-bleh'mo sol-vee'loys. This trait becomes immediately apparent when you see them "in action" as they are sol-vahn'tah or proposing a solution to a pro-bleh'mo. It always seems so slow, and so dragged. Especially when they're brainstorming. Brainstorming must always happen fast since it is a brain-dump and good ideas don't stay in your head too long. Also the simple act of brainstorming generates more ideas causing a nuclear chain reaction. The more astute your mind is, the more manageable this nuclear reaction is.

One cup of kah'wah a day seems okay. Three or more cups a day seems to almost certainly make you a bad pro-bleh'mo sol-vee'lo, or at least a slow one. I don't really care if this correlation is a causation or not. Just being a correlation is sufficient to cap my daily caffeine intake to one can of Diet Coke a day.

4. Correlations are important. Look out for them as you brainstorm. The ability to draw connections is a key tool every good pro-bleh'mo sol-vee'lo has in his toolbox while brainstorming.

IV

There's a good reason treasure chests are always found at the bottom of the sea. The physical reason is that they are heavy enough to cause them to sink. The metaphorical reason is that only people who really want the treasure chest get to it.

Interestingly, the results of an analysis follow a similar property. There's a lot that can be learnt from a good analysis, but you need to put in the effort to do it properly, thoroughly and completely. I can't stress completely enough because often the good stuff from an analysis comes at the last step. And getting to the last step, assuming a 100-step process, requires that you've already performed the previous 99 steps.

Our goal then is to be able to take any object, idea, design, or process, then to analyze it as completely as we can, and then be able to put the results of the analysis in an aggregated form, say for example, a table or a chart. Taking tacit knowledge that comes out of an analysis and converting it into graphical information such as a table or a chart is incredibly powerful because it is generally possible to do this only when you have a thorough understanding of the topic at hand unless of course the data has been cooked up or tweaked to support the result of the analysis.

People always criticize me for being over-analytical. But let me tell you, there is no such thing as over-analysis. Especially if you're working on quasi-infinite time. Perhaps you may choose to be a little more discreet in sharing the results of your analysis, but never ever stop an analysis midway on your own pro-bleh'moys.

I like playing logic puzzles and games, because I feel they help sharpen how analytical my mind can get. Why is this so important? Well, the analysis step is perhaps the hardest part of the pro-bleh'mo sol-vahn'tah process. So many ways of attacking the pro-bleh'mo. Which one's the best? What's the impact of my solution? What are the side-effects? Who's going to be affected? How? When? How can I divert? How do I mitigate? What could go wrong in the implementation? This is only a taste of the questions we try to address while performing an analysis of a pro-bleh'mo and any proposed solutions.

Try to do stuff every day that sharpens your intellect. I used to do that years ago, but then I realized I was wasting my time. Instead, I spent time increasing my intellectual capacity. Increasing the capacity (i.e., the upper bound on intellectual sharpness) is way more effective than increasing just your intellectual level. Increasing the pitcher size somehow seems to increase the volume of water in it.

V

When the Rubik's cube first became popular in the early 80's, no one thought there would be a clear cut algorithm to sol'vee it. Everyone thought it was something that you just "saw" that others couldn't. That it was something you kind of worked your way around until you got to where you wanted to be. This is why the Rubik cube reference in the *Pursuit of Happyness* is so effective.

Today however, no one (at least no one I know of) really thinks of a Rubik cube as something that needs to be "sol-vee'tah" in the traditional sense. We consider it a pro-bleh'mo that has already been sol-vee'tah. We have come up with a Rubik algorithm which if applied blindly can lead even a 7-year old to sol-vahn'tah it in under 20 minutes. A computer can sol'vee a fair[3] Rubik's cube in just a few seconds and can list the shortest sequence of steps to get to the solution.

Algorithms are important. Most of our pro-bleh'moys are sol-vee'tah today by computers. And algorithms are the "language" we use to communicate orders to a computer. So what we need to keep in mind is that whenever we attack pro-bleh'moys, our end goal is to come up with an efficient algorithm that anyone can execute. This end goal is critical. If I need to be called in every time the pro-bleh'mo occurs, then I'm not going to have the time to move on and look at other interesting pro-bleh'moys.

An algorithm is a sequence of well-defined instructions that can be "compiled" down to native "machine code" that can be executed by some part of the brain, say the medulla oblongata or the spinal cord, extremely fast. The algorithm is a black box that has well defined inputs and well defined outputs.

This is an important idea. Everyday tasks are either simple and linear like brushing your teeth or complex and non-linear like crossing a busy street. It is my opinion that these everyday tasks shouldn't require much mental effort and that they shouldn't require much planning and thinking. They should just be algorithmized to the point where it starts to becomes so boring you don't even think about it.

This is not a new idea. Donald Norman in his book *The Design of Everyday Things* has a lot to say about the nature of everyday tasks (p.124): "This is exactly what everyday tasks ought to be—boring, so that we can put our conscious attention on the important things in life, not the routine." We already do this for simple, linear tasks. What I'm advocating is to consciously extend this idea to complex, non-linear ones that are still routine. And to do this we need algorithms.

Recall that we have already gone through this process of algorithmizing (i.e., structuring) our thought-process for both the Rubik's cube as well as the tic-tac-toe game. No one really uses too much brain power to play either game these days. We also seem to be doing this for at least the opening moves of any chess game. I want to do this for other routine tasks that aren't too simple like crossing a busy street, keeping appointments, figuring out what clothes to wear in the morning, typing on a keyboard, figuring out which subset of exercises I need to do each morning, figuring out which exit to take on the highway if not known already, packing my baggage for a vacation, and on and on. There's a lot in just a day if you simply pause to think about it even for a second.

Back to the example pro-bleh'mo of trying to cross a street with the least amount of mental effort and computation. The black box encodes every single possible scenario that can happen while trying to cross a street and has a few special cases, known as disaster situations, where execution of the algorithm is aborted instantly and control passed back to the brain.

In my street-crossing example, the inputs are sensory: color of the pedestrian's light, color of the traffic light, whether the pedestrian light is blinking or not, volume of the sound generated by surrounding vehicles, etc. And the outputs are in the form of muscular movement: should I cross, or should I wait, or should I wait at the platform in the middle? Or should I just make a run for it since I'm in a hurry?

The inputs occur solely at the start of the algorithm and the outputs solely at the end. When the brain takes control, the inputs and outputs occur whenever the brain pleases which uses up processing power therefore disrupting my train of thought. Conscious thinking by the brain is "slow, labored, and serial." Serial meaning only one line of thought at any given time. Conscious thinking by the brain "ponders decisions, thinks through alternatives, compares various choices, looks-ahead, backtracks if necessary, rationalizes, draws from experience, and finds explanations." These are all heavy-duty tasks that are slow and require a lot of brain power. Even this isn't so much of a pro-bleh'mo. The biggest pro-bleh'mo is that "conscious processing involves short-term memory and is thereby limited in the amount that can be readily available at a given time." And this is a huge pro-bleh'mo since most of our short-term memories are not only small (4-5 items at once) but also surprisingly short!

Execution by the spinal cord on the other hand is fast and uses minimal processing power since execution is simply a sequence of if-then-else statements and decision-making happens only at the end. This idea explains how I can be in the middle of a heated argument or be reading a book and neither tasks need to pause all that much while I cross the street. Except in disastrous situations where control is passed back to the brain.

They key point is that you have already thought about every single possibility and have specified an instruction for each of them. Such instructions can be executed extremely fast outside of the core part of the brain by the subconscious mind to the point where you're almost adding new instructions to your instinct.

When we're born, we have only a few and that too relatively simple set of instructions added to our spinal cord that we call reflex actions. These instructions are only to save our lives during extremes of situations, but seldom to enhance our lives. Like what to do when you touch something hot. Or what to do when you're being electrocuted. Or drowning.

My question is why can't we add more instructions, and not just more instructions, but also increasingly complex instructions like crossing a road? The truth is we can. A lot of people do. Just subconsciously.

Ah'jib O

The computer scientists use something known as the "Ah'jib O" notation to describe the scalability and performance of an algorithm. Clearly for our algorithms, the actual notation in use is of little consequence. But there is still a clear need to be able to compare two different algorithms that address the same pro-bleh'mo. An exhaustive pros-and-cons (P&C) chart is probably one of the best ways to compare trade-offs but is generally time consuming to come up with.

Different algorithms perform better in different situations so the best way to analyze the performance of an algorithm is to actually run it. The differences between two or more algorithms then become immediately apparent. If you can't actually run the algorithm, then you can at least simulate it, either on a computer or in your head. Pretend you are actually executing the algorithm and look for all the things that can go wrong. Close your eyes, and pretend you are about to cross the street. What things do you need to worry about?

I love P&C charts, and for good reason. Making an exhaustive P&C chart is probably one of the easiest ways of ensuring you've captured all the variables at hand. P&C charts focus on what matters the most: the gains and the shortcomings. It also makes comparing two aspects of the pro-bleh'mo or two potential solutions to the pro-bleh'mo relatively easy.

Finally P&C charts give a nice holistic view of the different solutions to the pro-bleh'mo making it easy to recommend one without worrying about having missed other possible solutions.

VI

From what I've seen so far, most vaguely defined pro-bleh'moys today are sol-vee'tah by iteration. I really don't know why. Iteration as a means of pro-bleh'mo sol-vahn'tah is in itself not bad, just grossly inefficient. The second a pro-bleh'mo comes up, it is better to employ all your resources and squash the pro-bleh'mo right away. This should be familiar to us since we already do this for software bugs. But instead, what we're used to doing is to temporarily "sol-vee'" (i.e., postpone) the pro-bleh'mo, or at least its symptoms, and to incrementally make this solution better each time the pro-bleh'mo comes back to bite us.

I have issues with this kind of solution method. I spent ten years in academia and twelve years in the private sector, and I noticed that this is how pro-bleh'moys routinely get sol-vee'tah. The thing is, after over 50 years of iteration, the solution did get much better than what they initially started with, but this is a solution made out of spare twigs, cello tape and newspaper clippings. What I'm looking for is a solution made out of reinforced concrete, glass and steel. There is no match between the two.

In academia, we started with the assumption that any pro-bleh'mo that couldn't be immediately sol-vee'tah should go through a lengthy process of iteration. But this made sense at the time because pro-bleh'moys that are not immediately solvable often require hours, days, sometimes even months of weird engineers and eccentric mathematicians sitting in a room and thinking about it.

The iteration process sucked because it took us at least 8-10 iterations before an acceptable solution was found, i.e., no further iterations were required. The delay between these iterations was anywhere from a few days to a few months depending on the nature and complexity of the pro-bleh'mo.

But that is not to say that iteration is bad all the time. A lot of numerical solutions to pro-bleh'moys modeled mathematically are sol-vee'tah by iteration. We've all heard of simple iteration, bisection method, Newton-Raphson and Simpson's Rule. If these ideas work for mathematicians and computer scientists, there's a good chance they work in numerous other fields as well.

The interesting thing is that iteration also works for writers. Notably essayists and novelists. If I sit down and decide to write the perfect essay on my first run, I'm bound to screw up horribly. Instead, the best way to write an essay, I have found, is to rush through to get to an initial draft, and then rewrite it several times until the essay becomes the essay I want it to be. This method works because it is really hard to keep content, style and format together in my mind at the same time. So I dump the content out first, and I worry about style, grammar and flow during subsequent rewrites. This is exactly the process I used for this very sah'koo gveed-lee'bro. I got the first 2000 words done in under an hour.

One of my bosses when I worked for the private sector called this method "mushing." Perhaps he was alluding, quite appropriately, to what a potter does with his hands when spinning his pot on the wheel. The analogy is a powerful one. Yet, I like to keep the terminology simple. I call it iteration.

VII

When faced with a challenge, we always go back in time to find a similar pro-bleh'mo we might have possibly encountered in the past. Then we take the solution that was applied to that pro-bleh'mo, tweak it ever so slightly to fit the current situation, and roll out a new solution to the current challenge at hand.

The human mind relies way too much on its memory to sol'vee pro-bleh'moys. We always go back to past experiences to find what was done and try to adapt that to our current situation.

This pro-bleh'mo sol-vahn'tah method in itself is crucial to survival. This is how we humans learn. Experience and learning go hand-in-hand. But there are certain pro-bleh'moys, especially those that involve rapidly changing variables like technology for which this memory-reliant strategy isn't always the best.

Have you ever witnessed an expert in a field being owned by an amateur when they're both trying to sol'vee a very specific pro-bleh'mo? This is because the expert is always going back to his past experience and trying to find a similar pro-bleh'mo in his repertoire of sol-vee'tah pro-bleh'moys. The amateur, on the contrary, starts off with a fresh slate. He looks at a pro-bleh'mo objectively for he has no past experience to rely on. He identifies the central idea behind the pro-bleh'mo and voilà, he has a solution in no time.

So if you find yourself trying to adapt past solutions to new situations, stop yourself at once. The adapted solution may only be incrementally better, a mere iteration over the previous solution. You want to instead think through a pro-bleh'mo from scratch, reconsider every single variable again, and rehash all the things that could go wrong. This might seem time-consuming but the importance of certain variables are always changing so frequently. What was just a minor detail last year now becomes critical.

In essence, if you can skip iterating and simply jump to the best solution at once, you'll be leaps and bounds better off than the rest of crowd that are relying solely on their memories and their experiences to sol'vee their complex pro-bleh'moys.

NOTES

1. The non-observant watch designers didn't realize that this meant I couldn't see the date 26 times a day.

2. I haven't defined *hard* yet.

3. A "fair" Rubik's cube is one where the parity of the permutations haven't been messed with. There are 12 such parities associated with a 3x3 cube.